T0113529

What God has
Put
Asunder

What God has Put Asunder

Victor Epie'Ngome

Spears Books
Denver, Colorado

Spears Books
An Imprint of Spears Media Press LLC
7830 W. Alameda Ave, Suite 103-247
Denver, CO 80226
United States of America

First Published in the United States of America in 2021 by Spears Books
www.spearsmedia.com
info@spearsmedia.com
@spearsbooks

Information on this title: www.spearsmedia.com/what-god-has-put-asunder
© 2021 Victor Epie'Ngome
All rights reserved.

ISBN: 9781942876809 (Paperback)
ISBN: 9781942876816 (eBook)
Also available in Kindle format

Cover designed by Doh Kambem
Designed and typeset by Spears Media Press LLC

Distributed globally by African Books Collective (ABC)
www.africanbookscollective.com

For my children,
Nkwelle and Emuke

CONTENT

DRAMATIS PERSONNAE

WEKA: Young lady raised in an orphanage, wife to Garba. Proud, intelligent, respectful but toughened by Garba's dishonesty. Would do anything for her children.

GARBA: Weka's cheating husband. Takes other wives despite monogamous arrangement with Weka. Hypocrite politician and embezzling CEO of the community co-operative. Can't stand Weka questioning his squander mania

REV. GORDON: Expatriate rector of the orphanage, who gave Weka away in marriage to Garba. Hypocrite, he sexually exploited the girl entrusted to him, and has side flings with the nun who works with him.

SISTER SABETH: Rev. Gordon's compatriot, she is a nun working at the orphanage. Sabeth practically raised Weka. She is ignorant of what Gordon does to Weka until when the latter is about to leave the orphanage.

EMEKA: Suitor to Weka from neigbouring clan. Very hardworking and woke. Having grown up in the same orphanage, he knows Gordon and Sabeth well. His deliberate distortion of the language they taught him is his silent mockery of their conceit and the high ground on which they claim to stand.

CHILDREN: Where do children stand in a feud between their parents? Weka's children would not be pushed around by their father.

JUDGE: Hears the Garba versus Weka case. He is a no-nonsense judge but tends to leave things to time.

KINGE: Garba's party aide and confidant. Does most of Garba's dirty work, for what he can get out of him. A wheedling schemer.

FATOU: Garba's secretary and mistress, married to Sani, Garba's driver. Torn between loyalty to her husband and the pleasure of her secret escapades with Garba.

SANI: Fatou's husband and driver to Garba. He is industrious and trustworthy. Repairs watches to supplement his income as driver. But he could not resist Weka's determination to use him for her revenge against her husband's infidelity.

JIM RICAN: American businessman interested in buying produce from Weka's farms, and selling her some agricultural equipment.

IMPRESSARIO: A voice at the theatre

CAST OF THE FIRST RADIO PRESENTATION FOR RADIO NEDERLAND TRAINING CENTRE, HILVERSUM, HOLLAND, 1982

WEKA: Jiraporn Witayasakpan - Theatre Arts Lecturer, Chiang Mai University, Thailand

REV. GORDON: Gordon House – Producer, BBC World Service Drama, London. (Facilitator)

SISTER SABETH: Mavis Moyo – Radio producer, Harare, Zimbabwe

EMEKA: Gerry – BBC World Service Producer/Actor (Facilitator)

GARBA: Clairmont Taitt – Actor from Barbados

KINGE: Alos Yagas – Teacher from Papua New Guinea

FATOU: Mies – Actress, Holland

SANI: Askar Mehdi (Pakistan)

IMPRESSARIO: Flippe - Actor, Holland

STUDIO MANAGER: Freek Feenstra – RNTC, Hilversum, Holland

PRODUCTION SUPERVISOR: Gordon House, Richard Wade Actor /Trainer, UK

PRODUCER/ DIRECTOR: Victor EPIE'NGOME

FOREWORD

R eading *What God has Put Asunder* is a distressing experience. The forces of evil are all over, all powerful.

Weka, the victim, also appears like the source of her own problems but her naiveté is a silent appeal for our understanding and help. But as she ages, Weka grows wiser and stronger in character, backed up by children who know where to stand in an illegitimate union.

Victor Epie'Ngome is a Protestant with a strong Catholic background to which he retains an affectionate attachment. His choice of this Church to midwife Weka's initial corruption and subsequent tribulations is more to show the bumbling capability of such powerful institutions to wreak havoc despite the best intentions.

Talking of the Church, the entire work reminds me of a reading I heard at mass on the first Sunday of Lent, from the Book of Deuteronomy, which says:

My father was a wandering Aramaean. He went down into Egypt to find refuge. Few in numbers. Then he became a nation great, mighty and strong. The Egyptians ill-treated us. They gave us no peace and inflicted harsh slavery on us. But we called on the Lord, the God of our fathers. The Lord heard our voice and saw our misery, our toil and our oppression: and the Lord brought us out of Egypt with signs and wonders. He brought us here and gave us this land, a land flowing with milk and honey...

It amazes me still, that the Good Book should so completely cover all eventualities. May that Weka and her progeny savour a feast by the time V.E.N. is through with them.

Julius Wamey

PREFACE

Five years in Sasse College had endued me with a voracious appetite for reading. But Buea, in 1968, had no public library except that of the French Cultural Centre where, obviously, everything was in French. So, waiting for my GCE Ordinary Level results in Buea was a drill in intellectual starvation. Cornered by idleness, I fought back instinctively with... all I had - my pen. That is how my first play, *Musima my Son* was born. That play, whose manuscript I have since lost, won me the Radio Cameroon Drama Award that year - a prize no less valuable than a jumbo volume of *The Shorter Oxford English Dictionary*, which turned out a most subtle and enduring spur towards making word craft my lifetime stock-in-trade.

In my attempts to write, I drifted across a wide gamut of literary genres, with a rather perceptible penchant for verse. Then in 1981 the predicament of this not-altogether fictional lady called Weka got to me. It was the 20th anniversary of her marriage. Her husband had turned bestially abusive. His conscience was clearly dodging the column, and I could not but volunteer, with my pen once more, to try bringing him to quit playing ostrich.

Up till 10 p.m. every day the clatter of the keys of my old mechanical typewriter were the only sound to be heard on the first floor of the National Radio Station of Radio Cameroon where my office was found. In fact one day I got home to find a strange little note left by my younger sister, Sporah, and my cousin, Leopold, who were both living with me. It read 'Bro, hope you're fine. We miss you'. And they datelined it 'Hotel A7'. This was the number of my flat. We had not seen one another for two weeks in a row. By the time I got home from my writing, they had gone to bed, and when I woke up in the morning they had gone off to school.

Thus began my premature attempt to be delivered of a pregnancy which, it turned out, I would have to lug around for nearly a decade.

A year later, what I had written so far came in useful. I was attending a course in Radio Drama Production at the Radio Netherland Training Centre in Hilversum, Holland, and decided, for my end-of-course project, to do a condensed version of the play under the title *For Better or for Worse*. The play came very much alive thanks to the theatrical talent of my very close friend Jiraporn Witayasakpan, a Theatre Arts lecturer at Chiang Mai University in Thailand, and that of Clairmont Taitt, a born actor from Barbados. It was the first play I ever directed, and I had the benefit of expert mentoring from BBC World Service drama producer Gordon House, technical assistance from RNTC sound engineer, Freek Feenstra - a very lovable person, and some grudging assistance from Richard Wade.

Back home later that year, the play was broadcast on Radio Cameroon. My friends were prompt and unanimous in advising against a repeat broadcast - for my own safety, they said. And their advice was easy to take, for at least one key reason from my own side: I was not satisfied with the play. Something was missing, though I could not put my finger on it. So back into the drawer went tape and script - until six years later when I thought the last piece of the jigsaw had fallen into place and there was no point staying the delivery any further. I must also thank 'The Flame Players' troupe of Yaounde University for finally forcing the play out of the drawer. They came asking for permission to stage it, and I decided to coincide the publication with the opening night.

As I am about to publish it, I am reminded of my Art instructor who used to say, "never label your paintings, my boy, lest you write 'a cock' when you have painted a hen". And so let me just say that if this work were to be seen to stand on two solid feet - one literal and the other symbolic, such a bonus would make my day. And I hope that reading it, or eventually watching it on screen, will make yours.

What God has
Put
Asunder

ACT I

Scene 1

(Narrow orphanage room, Weka is lying on a small wooden bed, fast asleep. As curtain rises Sabeth enters the room, walks up to the bed, sits on its edge and shakes Weka gently).

SABETH

Weka...Weka! *(Weka opens her eyes)*
Wake up, my child.

WEKA

Hunh?
(Rubs her eyes violently, then tries to adjust them to the light)
Blessed Virgin! It's already morning?

SABETH

Seven o'clock, my dear. You missed morning devotion already, and you are just about to miss the most glorious sunrise of all time.

WEKA

(Tossing off the blanket)
I'm sorry, Sister Sabeth. I could hardly sleep all night. Just kept tossing and turning until the small hours of this morning.

SABETH

Anything the matter?

WEKA

I don't know, Sister. I just felt so low all night. As if something really depressing had just happened or was about to happen.

1

SABETH

You remembered to pray at least, I trust?

WEKA

Of course, yes. Many times. But it did not help. In fact I...I...I don't know.

SABETH

Oh, you'll be alright, my dear. Things like that happen to everybody. (*Pause*) I came to wake you because Reverend Gordon would like to see you. First thing this morning, he said.

WEKA

Rev. Gordon? Oh, my God, what does the rector want to see me so early for? What could it be?

SABETH

Well, I don't know if it's right for me to tell you. Maybe he should break the news himself.

WEKA

The news? What news? Sister Sabeth, please!

SABETH

Well, I suppose you will be sensible enough not to tell the Rector I told you.

WEKA

I will not tell him, Sister Sabeth, I swear....

SABETH

Tut! tut! tut! No swearing, my dear child. Just let your yes be yes and....

WEKA

I am sorry, Sister. I didn't mean to....

SABETH

The thing is, two men have been here to see the Rector?

WEKA

Two men! About me? What have I done to anybody?

SABETH

You did nothing my dear.

WEKA

Then who are these men, and what could they want with me? I
don't even know any....

SABETH

But they seem to know you very well. One of them says he is your
cousin.

WEKA

My cousin? But, Sister Sabeth, you know very well I have no rela-
tives. Otherwise my father would not have left me in the orphanage
before he died.

SABETH

I know. But this fellow comes from the Njanga clan as well....

WEKA

I am Njanga, yes, but that does not make him my....

SABETH

Well, I thought in Africa everybody is everybody's cousin, brother,
sister, uncle, aunt, father, mother.

WEKA

(A little sour)

I know, Sister Sabeth. But what will this particular cousin want
with me now, is my problem.

3

SABETH

It happens that my little Weka is a well-brought-up girl with a rather ungodly allowance of good looks, and Garba happens to be particularly sensitive to fresh beauty.

WEKA

(Rather reproachfully)
Sister Sabeth *(pause)*. And his name is Garba?

SABETH

Yes. Miché Garba.

WEKA

Sounds like the herdsman turned businessman cum politician.

SABETH

That's right. I thought you would know him. There seem to be very few people around here who don't.

WEKA

You said there was a second man.

SABETH

Yes, he comes from the neighbouring Delta clan. He has a tongue-twisting name.

WEKA

Delta - the land of tinkers.

SABETH

(Nods assent)

WEKA

I hear there isn't a single corner of the globe where you won't find a Deltan tinkering or selling something.

SABETH

You may have been too young to notice, but your people and the Deltans lived practically together for a long time.

WEKA

I hear there are still many Deltans here. Too many, I should say.

SABETH

Too many? You sound xenophobic, Weka.

WEKA

No. Just that they seem to fill the whole place. The Deltans have replaced the roosters in our clan, I hear. It's a Deltan who wakes you up in the morning, shouting and clattering pieces of tin - to get an old bucket or pot to mend. No sooner does that one leave than another comes hollering, a sewing machine on his shoulder, wanting to mend your old clothes.

SABETH

That's Delta all right. Smart and enterprising people. And it would appear this one is a particularly successful man.

WEKA

(Laughing)
I never knew you like this, Sister Sabeth. Now you look and sound like a match maker of some sort.
(Both laugh briefly, then pause)

SABETH

Well, maybe I should tell you that the Delta one also grew up here in the orphanage.

WEKA

Oh!

SABETH

Yes, and you know him very well. *(Triumphant smile)*
It's your friend Emeka.

WEKA

(Excited) Oh! Emeka! I didn't remember he was Deltan. What
brings him back here? Did he and...and the other man come
together?

SABETH

You must be kidding. Two suitors for the same woman coming
together?

WEKA

(Disappointed and worried) Suitors? I said it! I said something
nasty was in the offing.

SABETH

Something nasty? Why do you talk like that, Weka?... Well, this
is why I ought to have left this whole business to the Rector....
Listen, I'll leave you to say your prayers and tidy yourself up. I'll
be back in twenty minutes to fetch you. Hurry up, the Rector has
been waiting too long already.

*Exit Sabeth. Weka drops on her knees by the bedside and prays
in inaudible mumbles.*

Curtain

❋ ❋ ❋

Scene 2

(Rector's office. Gordon is seated at the table, draped in a white cassock. He is typing on an old typewriter, between sips of tea. Sabeth is sitting on the only spare chair, cleaning the crucifix of her rosary with a white handkerchief. Weka is half leaning, half perched on a high stool, manifestly disillusioned).

GORDON
(Suddenly stopping and raising his face towards Weka)
Yes, my child, I'm listening. *(long pause)* Weka, I hope you are not feeling unloved, or unwanted. In fact, I meant to tell you, in a very personal way, how proud I am of you. You have been a most exemplary girl. I don't mind telling you to your face that, among your peers, you have been the showpiece of this orphanage (if I may use so worldly a term as 'showpiece'). Both Sister Sabeth and I are most aggrieved by the prospect of your eventual departure from these precincts. But the Lord clearly has another corner for you to brighten, and we have no doubt whatever that you are up to the task.

WEKA
You are very kind, Reverend Gordon, and I cannot but bow to the will of the Almighty. But can it only be through marriage?

GORDON
I am so delighted you are able to read between the lines. But listen, my child. God made Adam happy in the garden, but soon realised he needed a companion. So, He....

WEKA
So He caused a deep sleep to fall on him.... Now that you mentioned that... *(Apologetic)* I'm sorry to interrupt you, Reverend, but how could God only be realising Adam's loneliness afterwards? What happened to His all-pervading foreknowledge?

GORDON

(Looks at Sabeth. Both nod, apparently impressed with the question).

That, my dear, is a most intelligent question, which we surely have to find time to dig into. But as I was saying, God made Eve out of Adam's bone, and....

WEKA

And commissioned man and woman to leave their parents and cling to each other. That is one of the most elementary things I learnt during my catechumen days. But, Reverend, how do I cling to one or the other of two complete strangers?

GORDON

(Derisive smile) Well, what about Sister Sabeth and me? We are strangers too. Even more strangers than....

WEKA

Maybe you were when I was brought to this orphanage as a child. But now I have come to know you.

GORDON

That's exact, my child. There is not a soul in this orphanage that has not drawn from your boundless capacity to love. And I am persuaded you can get around to loving anyone and anything.

WEKA

(Losing her temper) Thank you for all that, Reverend Gordon, if it is intended as a compliment. But let us not beat about the bush. If you have had enough of me in this orphanage...just come out with it and I'll go out and be by myself. Thanks to the education I have received from you, I am very sure I can fend for myself. Really, you needn't fear for me at all.

SABETH

You cannot talk like that, Weka.

WEKA

How else am I to talk, Sister Sabeth? It was you who told me that my father got killed while fighting against the Germans - defending a crown he knew nothing about; in a war that was none of his business - and that my mother died before I could even talk.

GORDON

Weka, it was I who administered extreme unction to your mother. And when she handed you over to me, she made me also promise that as soon as you were of age, I would make sure you were married. So it is completely out of the question for you to talk of being by yourself.

WEKA

So the choice has to be between two complete strangers?

GORDON

Garba and Emeka are not such strangers after all. They are Africans just like you. What do you mean?

SABETH

And not only African. Garba is of the Njanga clan like you, and Emeka is....

WEKA

You told me that before, Sister Sabeth. But didn't you also tell me that back in your native England a girl only marries the man she loves?

SABETH

Yes, but that's in England.

GORDON

Listen, Weka, it took us centuries to establish all those civilities, and this is a totally different setting. This is Africa, for God's sake.

WEKA

(A touch of contumacy in her tone) Of course, Reverend Gordon.
How could I have forgotten that? Hasn't Sister Sabeth always
reminded me how primitive we are?

GORDON

Shut up Weka. You are being rude.

SABETH

And that's an insult to your education, Weka. What a shame!

WEKA

(Very angry) Maybe it is. But tell me this, Reverend Gordon; when
you first came to this land-of-no-civilities, weren't you told that a
girl never knew a man until she got married?

SABETH

(Intervening) Weka! O my God!

WEKA

Weka! O your God! Wasn't it you, Sister Sabeth, who taught me
everything I know?

SABETH

And the Lord Himself knows I was as liberal as I could be with
your education, but....

WEKA

But what, Sister Sabeth? Didn't you tell me, as part of that same
liberal education, that a girl insulted her family if the sheet on her
bridal bed gave away any premarital traffic? Didn't you....

GORDON

I order you to shut up, child!

WEKA
(Derisive laughter) Of course, you do. That's all it takes - an order, and the Rector's holy will is done. Aren't you lucky?

SABETH
I'm sorry, Reverend Gordon, I must leave now.
(Rises to leave)

WEKA
(Rising and standing in her way)
No, you're not going anywhere, Sister Sabeth. I want you to stay here and see Reverend Gordon browbeat me into marrying against my will.
(Mimicking Gordon) I order you to shut up, child!... Do you take your children to b...I mean, when you used to call me up to clean the mission house, and then drag me into your bedroo....

GORDON
(Very embarrassed) Weka, get out of this office! Immediately!

WEKA
Easy, easy! You don't need to shout...but you must answer me, before I go. Was that liberal education, or was it libertine?

SABETH
Please, Weka my darling, I have always told you never to allow anger to control you. Come, let's go.
(Leads Weka to the door.)
Rev. Gordon, I think you can leave Weka to me.
(Leaves Weka at the door and walks back a few steps to whisper to Gordon).
You see, we must do it without seeming to push her.

GORDON
The child is in a queer mood. You must make her say her Act of Perfect Contrition.

WEKA

(Turning violently to address Gordon).
Aren't you a great one for saving souls? In any case, I know any
time I am in need of a shrift I can simply repair to the Reverend
Rector's bedroom.
(Mimicking Gordon)
You must make her say her act of....

SABETH

(Interrupting and shoving her out) Sssh! Don't, my dear. You must
not talk back to the Rector. That breeds bad luck. You know he is
like your father now.
(Closes door. They walk a few steps)
But… Weka, is … is it true?

WEKA

What?

SABETH

That Reverend Gordon took you to...I mean...are you no longer
a virgin?
*(Weka drops her face, remains quiet for a long while, then
snatches a handkerchief from Sabeth and takes it to her eyes).*
O my God!

Curtain

✳ ✳ ✳

ACT II

Scene 1

(A room in a luxury hotel. Splashing of water in the bathtub offstage left. Garba, dressed in gandura, is seated in a sofa downstage right, putting on his socks between sips of tea to which he adds some whisky).

FATOU
(Calling from offstage left)
Garba!

GARBA

What now?

FATOU
Pass me my towel, please, darling. I forgot to take it.

GARBA
(A bit irritable) Where is it?

FATOU
In the wardrobe. Near my make-up box.

GARBA
(Rummages in wardrobe downstage centre, finds the towel and takes it to bathroom door downstage left. Knocks and opens door at the same time. Standing in the doorway, he holds out the towel).

GARBA

Here you are. I hope that will be it.

FATOU

Thank you, my dear. I don't think I shall bother you any....

GARBA

But the hotel always provides towels. Why do you insist on bringing yours along?

FATOU

I told you I never use hotel towels. Some look clean, but they are
not always safe. And, by the way, this is the last time we come to
this hotel.

GARBA

And why?

FATOU

No hot water in the bath.

GARBA

What do you want hot water for? It's so hot and sticky outside.
Even the water is not cold.

FATOU

Not only that. It's too near.

GARBA

Fatou my dear, Satellite Hotel has the highest standing in town.
Where else do you want to go?

FATOU

Out of town, of course. We can't both be leaving our homes and
spending nights in hotels in the same town. Suppose one of your
wives gets to know?

GARBA

My wives don't care. They know I have prerogatives as a man.

FATOU

And what about my husband?

GARBA

He likes driving for me, and I guess even if he knew, he would keep his beak shut. Otherwise he would have only his watch repairing to live on.

FATOU

Man, it's my husband you are talking about.

GARBA

Woman, it's your boss you are talking to.
(Quickly changing to a soothing tone)
But this is a boss who loves you. Makes all the difference, doesn't it? *(Pause)* Angry? I thought it was a draw.

FATOU

I'm sorry I'll bother you once again. Could you fetch me the slippers, please?

GARBA

(Takes off his own slippers and shoves them across to Fatou)
Here, take mine. And please, don't stay in that bathroom forever. I would like to look at the speech.

FATOU

(Comes out, wrapped up to her breast in a large towel).
Suppose, Garba that I was your wife?

GARBA

You think if we were married I would still love you so much after all these years? No way. A wife is a different kettle of fish, you know.

That's why, even after my next wife comes in tomorrow, *(he puts his arms about her)* you and I will always be like this - very special. *(He kisses her while she is half-heartedly pushing him away).*

FATOU

(Once released, slaps Garba lightly on cheek and walks towards the wardrobe).
Your speech is all typed. The stencils are in the big leather bag in here *(pointing to the wardrobe).* I'll get them for you if....

GARBA

No, that's alright. I'll get them while you go and get dressed
(Opens wardrobe and starts searching while Fatou exits right. After a while of rummaging and grumbling, he finds the stencils, then rehearses the speech.)
Comrades, I know your cherished dream, because it has also been my dream. We have all been dreaming of the ultimate departure of the colonial bug who sucked our economy dry. We've been dreaming of the day when, in the concert of free nations, our voice too could be heard and respected. That dream has become reality. That day is here. We have crossed the Red Sea. Looking at what our neighbours are doing, you would have reason to fear that this freedom was not worth praying for; reason to look back towards Egypt with regret rather than forward with hope. You will see the toiling masses continuing to eke out a wretched existence, while a few opportunists bloat themselves up and wallow in ill-gotten lux... *(stops to correct something)* ill-gotten lux....

FATOU

(Interrupting, still offstage right)
Did you find them?

GARBA

What? Oh yes *(Resumes reading)*...ill-gotten luxury. They hoard away the people's hard-earned resources in fabulous bank accounts and mansions in foreign lands. The only thanks the people get for voting them into power is the mud they splash on them as they zoom past in the limousines bought with their very taxes. The litany of social injustices is endless.

But we mean it to be different here in Njanga. The road to the promised land is long and rugged but we shall trudge along together, sharing bread and water in brotherhood....

FATOU

(Softly) I hope I did not mess up the script.

GARBA

Not at all, darling. The typing's superb. Just one or two minor corrections. Do you think you can manage to rush to the party headquarters and run them off?

FATOU

(Thinking) The luncheon is in an hour. Yes, I think there's enough time. How many copies?

GARBA

Er...let me see... Run off about...50? No, that's too much. Most of them are illiterates. 20 will do. (Phone rings. He picks up the receiver). Yes, hello!... Speaking. Ah, comrade Kinge, you sound like you have a cold... That's right, the campaign trail has been very dusty. Well, we had no choice. The campaign would not have got anywhere in the rainy season... Comrade Kinge, I appreciate all those sacrifices you are making, and you can be sure when it's all over, you will not regret it one bit... Already! How many of them?... OK, tell them I will be down in a jiffy... Yes. OK.

(Hangs up. Fatou dashes about as she prepares to leave).

FATOU

Where is Kinge calling from?

GARBA

From the conference room. All my campaign aides are there. I've got to go down at once.

(Exiting right).

You can take any of the party cars. And the party drivers.

(Pokes his head back in and addresses Fatou with a smile) ...and do me a favour, will you?

FATOU

What now?

GARBA

Don't wear yourself out. Try to stay fresh for me, OK?

FATOU

(Nods)

Don't work too hard, you too.

(Exit Garba, followed shortly by Fatou)

Curtain

* * *

Scene 2

(Mission house, Rev. Gordon, in pyjama trousers, his torso bare, with towel slung over his shoulder, is pouring tea from a flask, whistling. There is a knock. Gordon opens the door and Sabeth enters left. Noticing Gordon, she moves back).

SABETH

Sorry, Reverend Gordon, I can wait outside until you're dressed.

GORDON

Don't be ridiculous, Sabeth. I opened without asking because I knew it was you. Hop in, my love. Why did you choose to knock this time?

SABETH

(Recoiling)
Please, take your hands off me. I came to talk to you about Weka.

GORDON

I see. About how much libertine education I have been giving her in my bedroom.

SABETH

About who of the suitors will down the dregs of the holy wine.

GORDON

Please, Sabeth, spare me that, will you?

SABETH

I don't blame you though. If I were a man myself, I would definitely prefer something fresh and juicy like Weka - to a warped and withered old museum artefact like Sabeth.

GORDON

Don't tell me you believe all that hogwash Weka was talking in that office. I mean don't you see she felt cornered and frustrated, and had to get back at someone?

SABETH

Well, who is better placed to interpret her moods? You seem to know her inside out. Anyhow, she is going.

GORDON

I know she is supposed to be going.

SABETH

Too bad for everybody, isn't it? Especially for some.

GORDON

Believe what you will, Sabeth, but you don't have to go on about it forever.

SABETH

Go on about what? I am speaking in earnest. I really think this orphanage got more out of Weka than it put into her.

GORDON

(After a brief pause) Well, has she chosen?

SABETH

She has capitulated. You cannot sincerely talk of choosing, let's face it. She hasn't met either suitor properly. She knows stories about both, but that's hearsay.

GORDON

So what did she say?

SABETH

Seems persuaded that Garba is the lesser of two evils.

GORDON

Garba, that's the politician.

SABETH

Right.

GORDON

Not bad; I mean, if he is really the sort of man that comes across in his speeches then Weka will have no cause to regret her choice.

SABETH

I do hope for her sake that he is not just one of these sweet-talking public figures who can't even run a home properly. You know orphans are rather sensitive people. I mean Weka....

GORDON

(Cutting her short)
Darling, if that's her choice I guess they will know how to sort it out. We shall have done our duty, shan't we?
(Reaches out towards her but she withdraws and is about to go out).

SABETH

You are right. My last duty was to inform the Rector about her decision, and I have just done so. Now I must leave.

GORDON

(Standing in her way)
Come on, don't be like that.

SABETH

Like what? I should not stand in your way. In a short while Weka will be gone for good. Remember this is an orphanage, and it will be ages before you have another fresh, full-bosomed thing like her. Enjoy yourself, man.

GORDON

Sabeth!
(They struggle at the door, she to go out, he to prevent her).

Curtain

❋ ❋ ❋

Scene 3

(Campaign grounds. Garba addresses rally using a microphone. Crowds are cheering as curtain rises).

GARBA

You know, ladies and gentlemen, there cannot be peace unless we can share bread. Why are governments falling everyday? Why are people fighting everywhere? How can there be peace and concord if some starve while others waste? What happiness can there be in a home where the woman works and the husband squanders the money living it up with prostitutes? (*Applause*) Dear comrades, we have a battle to fight, and we shall win. Against tribalism...bribery and...corruption and neo-colonialism!

Comrades, the People's party is committed to winning this fight, and the coming election is your chance to ensure that victory, because it will be YOUR victory, Long live the people's party!

(Prolonged applause and shouts of 'victory' and 'long live' from the crowd. Kinge mounts the rostrum and walks up to the microphone.)

KINGE

Ladies and gentlemen, dear comrades; it is a big honour for me, in proposing this toast to the inevitable victory of the people's party, to announce on the same august occasion the enlargement of our sole candidate's family. Our dear and most honourable Miché Garba here will be taking in a brand new wife in the next twenty-four hours. Ladies and gentlemen, let's drink to the new conquest.

(Applause and clinking of glasses with shouts of 'Hear! Hear!')

Curtain

✳ ✳ ✳

Scene 4

(In Church. Weka and Garba are kneeling at the altar in wedding attire. Father Unor thumbs through the pages of a big Bible.)

UNOR

Oremus in nomine patris, et filii, et Spiritu Sanctu.

CONGREG

Amen.

UNOR

Brothers and sisters in Christ, we are all here today to witness the tying of a knot. Weka has been a most active member of this congregation, and has paid all her contributions. Today she stands before you to solicit your prayers and God's blessings for a new life bond with Miché Garba, kneeling here to my left. Before this assembly I ask: Who is it that gives this woman in marriage to this man?

GORDON

Upon the mandate of her deceased mother, and on behalf of the All Saints Union orphanage which brought her up, I do.

UNOR

Does anyone here object to this marriage? *(Silence)* Let them speak now or forever hold their peace. *(pause)* Well, if there is no objection....

EMEKA

(Raises a finger quickly in the crowd)
I am objection it, Sah.
(Walks vigorously up the aisle as crowd murmur. Then silence).

UNOR

Well, who are you, Sir?

EMEKA

Eh? Look at me proper. If you does not conconise me then you are suffer magnesia. Anyway, my nomination is Emeka. Emeka Nwachukwu of Umudele, Delta clan.

UNOR

And what is your objection, Mr Em....Emeka Nwa....nwa...God help me.

EMEKA

This woman are my woman.

UNOR

And how is that, please?

EMEKA

How like how? She are my woman, that's all Matrimonically, financically, domestically she are my woman. You can ask the interrogation for Reverend Gordon who is stooding by your side there.

UNOR

(*Turning to Gordon*) Reverend Gordon?

GORDON

I do in no wise stand by that claim.

EMEKA

Hear how you de talk now, Reverend Gordon. This girl growed in the orphanage under your care.

GORDON

Yes.

EMEKA

And I growed in the same orphanage under your care, though I older than she and I vacated from the orphanage before she do.

GORDON

All of that is true, gentleman, but I don't see how it makes Weka your wife. I know you got along very well while in the orphanage, but that was as childhood friends.

EMEKA

What are you mean by childhood friends? In the African customary, woman are friend to woman and man are friend to man. Man are not friend to woman. If man get along to woman, as you call it, and she are not his sister, she are his wife or intendant.

GORDON

Whatever be the provisions of your strange..."customary" or whatever you call it, don't forget that you and Weka were both children being brought up together in the orphanage.

EMEKA

(*Long derisive laugh*) Reverend Gordon, so you have resident in Africa for so many ages of years and yet you does not know that Africa marriage start in the childhood? Is it because of dowry or.... as you calls it, pride brice? When I was still a childhood my papa for givam, even if it was quantums of cows and goats. But even as he was not alive, Chineke keep his dear soul, I for do it myself when I growed up small. Only she too have no father, and I cannot give the dowry pride bride to you since you....

GORDON

This is the 20th century, Emeka, and childhood marriages arranged by parents are not part of civilised living. I brought you up and I am ashamed you don't recognise that.

EMEKA

I coconise well well that you does not like this kind marriage in your country fashion. Thas why I am not pay pride...dowry for you. But Weka is Africa woman and I am Africa man. And marriage of Africans must to follow according by African customary country fashion, not English civilisation.

And you say that you bring us up. Yes. And thas why she have better chance to understanding me than any other man. We have growed up with the same thinking and the same fashion. Look at herself. She fever me and I fever she.

GORDON

I'm afraid, Mr. Emeka, you should have sorted out your claims before now. It's rather late. But, as you know, the courts are still open even after we conduct this marriage. And let me remind you that Weka chose Garba of her own free will.

EMEKA

Which free wheel? Have she become an engineerer?

GORDON

I'm sorry, Mr Emeka, we'll have to proceed. Make an effort to be a cheerful loser.

EMEKA

God punish you for your chairful loser. You think I have transversal the Cross River to proceed here because I have no chairs in my house? Look, my friend, if you do not take your kiaful, I am not mind to interfere this bloody cerebellum now.

(pause)

GORDON:

(*Sighs*) May we proceed, Mr Emeka?

EMEKA

(*Moving away angrily*) Ngwanu, you may proceed. Only because I respect church

(*Turns to warn*) But one day we shall visualise who be who. All those cunny-cunny which you people are doing in confidential will composed in opendential. It is me, Emeka Nwachukwu of Umudele Delta who have spoke it.

(*Disappears into the crowd*)

UNOR

(*Sigh of relief*) Would the bridegroom, please, step forward? (*pause as she does*)

Do you, Miché Garba, take this woman, Weka, as your wife, to love and to cherish, to have and to hold; to honour....

GARBA

Yes, but not to obey, Reverend Unor. I cannot obey a woman.

UNOR

I have not finished, Mr Garba.

GARBA

D'accord! D'accord. Yes, I do.

UNOR

Well, why don't you let me finish?

GARBA

Doesn't matter. You are busy, I am busy, everyone is busy. And we have already lost much time with this debate over...just forget it. Yes, I do.

UNOR

Weka, do you accept Miché Garba as your wedded husband, to love and to cherish, to have and to hold, to honour and obey, in sickness or in health, for richer or for poorer, for better or for worse? If so be your decision, say, 'yes, I do'.

(*Long pause. Weka remains silent, her head bowed*)

SABETH

(*In a reproachful whisper*) Weka, please, say something. Please, don't embarrass us.

WEKA

(*Struggling not to cry*)
But I don't even know the man, Sister Sabeth.

SABETH

Please, darling, let's not start this all over again. What is so hard in just saying 'yes, I do'?

WEKA

(*Raises her head and looks at Garba, then shakes her head*) Sister Sabeth, something tells me I can't trust this man. (*pause*) I just wonder if someone here cares what happens if he turns mean later. What seems to matter is for me to say 'yes, I do'. Okay, yes, I do.

(*Unor beckons Gordon and Sabeth aside and they confer while the crowd murmur and fidget. Then Unor moves back to centre of the altar*)

UNOR

Considering the rather unusual circumstances of this ceremony, notably the reluctance with which the bride gave her consent, and the fact that the groom took exception to certain portions of the marriage vow - an attitude which may be deemed to justify the fears expressed by the bride - we had a mind to cancel or defer the marriage. (*Murmur*) But as this would mean keeping a grown-up girl in the orphanage again for...God alone knows how long, we have deemed it proper to solemnise this marriage on probation. (*prolonged murmurs*) Yes, we shall withhold the rings. The couple shall live as they please for ten years, during which time they should get to know each other properly. If they confirm their desire to continue as a couple after this period, then we shall complete today's ceremony by putting these rings on their fingers. On these terms we now declare Miché Garba and Weka husband and wife. In nomine Patri et Filii et Spiritu Sanctu.

CONGREG

Amen.

(*Choir sings or organ plays wedding march as curtain falls slowly*)

ACT III

Scene 1

(Garba's secretariat. Fatou is typing. Door opens and Garba enters. He walks up to Fatou).

GARBA

How is ma Cherie today?
(Tries to kiss her. Fatou holds him off gently and is slightly reproachful)

FATOU

The door is open.
(She goes to close it. In the meantime, Garba examines some papers on her desk)

GARBA

Another hotel bill? Who's this from?

FATOU

(Coming back and sitting down)
Satellite. Who else?

GARBA

How much? Let's see...300,000 CFA...for four days. Not that bad.
Fatou, write a cheque and bring it to me for signature.

FATOU

On which account? The private or the Co-operative's

GARBA

The Co-operative's, of course.

FATOU

Again?

GARBA

What do you mean? What am I General Manager for? Must the institution live on the man and not the man on the institution?

FATOU

I just fear it is a little too much. Suppose the auditors....

GARBA

The what? Don't the auditors know that a cow can only browse within the reach of its tether? Auditors them too no de chop? And by the way, who commissions the auditors. They can only check what I ask then to check.

FATOU

But there is hardly anything left in the Co-op's account.

GARBA

The Co-operative has far broader shoulders, my dear.

FATOU

I'm not sure I understand that.

GARBA

It's simple. The Co-op is everybody and nobody. So its losses weigh on no one in particular, because they are shared by all the members.

FATOU

But the members may not all just bear the losses with a patient shrug. Somebody somewhere will be digging into how they came about. That may mean probing the management, and I'm afraid of what may happen if the mistletoe is found to survive the tree.

GARBA

You are certainly taking too much liberty there, Fatou. However, the mistletoe dies with the tree only if it did not propagate its seeds to other trees. And in any case, this is not the co-op's account.

FATOU

I agree, but I'm simply afraid. They say many days for the thief, but.

GARBA

I don't know who your thief is but, please, write out the cheque and let me sign before I leave for the meeting.

FATOU

Oh, I forgot there was a letter too.
(Hands it to Garba who tears it open and reads, still standing)

GARBA

(Reading) 'I have the honour to tender herewith my...' Fatou, what is happening? Why is Sani doing this just when I am considering him for a raise? He is the best driver this company has. Does he know about us?

FATOU

(Writing out the cheque) I don't know. But I doubt it.

GARBA

I hope not, because that would be terrible. It would be scandals without end, especially now that my youngest wife is also beginning to act up.

FATOU

Maybe you should stop seeing me.

GARBA

Don't be ridiculous, Fatou.

(*Reads amount on cheque*)

Three hundred thousand. (*Signs*) Here you are. Tell the accountant to charge it to... (*thinks for a while*) What Head now?... Let him charge it to 'Miscellaneous'. Sub-head: 'Representation'. Okay? And I'll be seeing you tonight.

FATOU

And suppose your wife wants to come to the show?

GARBA

She won't. She doesn't even know what theatre is. Are there theatres in the orphanage? (*They laugh*) Okay, I have to go now. The meeting will last all day. But don't forget tonight. (*From the doorway*) I'll pick you up at the usual place.

Curtain

✳ ✳ ✳

Scene 2

(*Little shed by the roadside. Sani is busy cleaning out a watch. Enter Weka*)

SANI

(*With affected formality*)

Can I be of help, Madame le Directeur?

WEKA

Yes, please. My watch, it stopped.

SANI

(Takes the watch and examines it)
A very fine quartz watch. What is wrong with it? *(pause)* But...
What are you complaining about? It works perfectly well.

WEKA

(Hushed and very familiar tone)
Sani, forget the watch. *(Smiles)* Wasn't sure of meeting you. No
work today?

SANI

No. No more. I have resigned.

WEKA

What? Don't be ridiculous.

SANI

Honest. I tendered it this very morning.

WEKA

Why, Sani? I thought you needed the job.

SANI

I did at one time. But now I need something else more.

WEKA

Always something new, Sani. What is it this time?

SANI

My freedom, my time. Time to be home. Time to see more of
you. Now, don't get me wrong. Your husband has been a good
boss. Which is why I worked there for the past sixteen years. But
I think I am past the age for being tossed about, sent on all sorts of
errands, many of which entail spending weeks away from home.
And all that for what? Bird shit.

WEKA

And now; you hope to survive on this watch repairing?

SANI

I was repairing watches before I got that job. If I didn't starve to death then, I don't think I will now.

WEKA

But Sani, times have changed. This is no longer the age of hair-springs and balance wheels. Everybody is going quartz. And as you know, most electronic watches are so cheap that when something goes wrong people would much rather replace than repair them.

SANI

Well, dear, you cannot eat your cake and have it, can you? I have opted for what I deem more precious and I don't mind paying the price

WEKA

And your wife?

SANI

What about her? She likes her job, and I think it is a help. Except that I see less and less of her. But that also gives me time to be with you.

WEKA

(In a whisper)

Don't look at me like that with all these snoopy eyed people passing so close. Keep fiddling with the watch. Is she home now?

SANI

Who? Fatou? Yes, but she is leaving in about an hour. Going to the village. Says her mother is taken ill. May be back tomorrow or later.

WEKA

Perfect timing.... Well, I mean... if you'd like to go with me.

SANI

Go with you? Where to?

WEKA

Tonight's show. The play at the Capitol. The Ivory Productions Association are staging 'Herod Antipas'

SANI

Beautiful play, I hear.

WEKA

Coming, aren't you?

SANI

But...but what about your husband?

WEKA

Won't be around either. Told me nothing, but I saw his bag packed. He certainly is about to travel.

SANI

And suppose he cancels?

WEKA

I'm sure he won't. But if he does, I'll let you know at once.

SANI

What time's the show?

WEKA

9 p.m. prompt.

SANI

Okay, at eight I'll call you from a friend's.

WEKA
You can't do that, Sani. Suppose....

SANI
Don't you worry, my dear. It will be just a signal. I'll let the phone ring twice. You don't need to answer if...the coast is clear, as we used to say in school.

WEKA
And if it is not?

SANI
If you have to answer, say something like...like...sorry, sir, you have got the wrong number'

WEKA
And if he gets the phone before I do?

SANI
Same thing. Wrong number.

WEKA
(Takes back her watch and straps it about her wrist)
Okay, old fox, I buy that. *(Hands him an envelope)* Here, take this.

SANI
What? Not again, Weka. You don't need to give me the money. I can take you out this once. Really, I can afford it.

WEKA
I know you can. Even if you have been paid your benefits, I still would rather you have this money than let him give it away to street girls. I'll see you tonight.
(Hails a taxi)

Taxi!

SANI

See you, darling.

WEKA

(As taxi pulls up)
Taxi, Lake Residence, please.
(Get's into cab and it drives off).

Curtain

✳ ✳ ✳

Scene 3

(Garba's plush sitting room).

GARBA

(Shouting) You are overstepping your bounds, Weka!

WEKA

I am not, Garba. I am operating perfectly within the bounds of
our marriage arrangement.

GARBA

The arrangement for me to obey you, isn't it?

WEKA

(Sarcastic)
No, the arrangement for you to cheat and neglect me. For you to
spend weeks living it up in hotels with harlots or... or whatever,
while I sit in your house like a piece of furniture, watching the
arms of the clock till I get dizzy; waking up alone every morning

to resume measuring out my suffering with a teaspoon.

GARBA

But you know my job, Weka. You shouldn't talk like that.

WEKA

Of course, I shouldn't. Am I not married to the only Managing Director and honourable parliamentarian? But I happen to know that parliament is people. That politics is all about people. About families too. And what kind of politician is it who cannot look after his family?

GARBA

Shut up, woman. It's enough now. Do you hear me? Enough! A man returns to his house, can't have a little bite to eat....

WEKA

Oh yes, of course, a bite to eat. That's what I came here to become - a cook. And yet, how many times a week do I stay awake till late in the night warming supper which you never come home to eat?

GARBA

(*Shaking his head in frustration*) I...I don't know what's wrong with you. Your mouth is full of invective. It's as if I were not your husband. I mean...you should....

WEKA

I should crawl. I should creep into my dear honourable Sir Oracle and thank him with whispering humbleness for treating me like... like a concubine, and my children like bastards.

GARBA

(*Grumbling*)

Just a chance! Just give her a split chance to get started and there is no stopping the avalanche. (*To Weka*) Weka, do you realise you are not my only wife? Your mates never question what I do, but you....

WEKA

That's their funeral. I was brought up to ask questions about everything I don't understand. You should have known that before saying your hasty 'Yes I do'. (*Snatches his handbag*) Now let me see what's in here.

GARBA

Look! Look, Weka, leave my.... let me have that bag back immediately! (*Struggling for it*) Gi...gi...give it to me! I say give it to me!

WEKA

I won't!

GARBA

Look, don't open that bag, Weka!
(*Weka snaps zipper open*)
I say, Weka, stop it. You have no right!

WEKA

(*Rummaging in the bag*)
I haven't, have I?
(*Takes out a cheque booklet and throws the bag to him*)
There! Take your bag.
(*Reads some cheque stumps*)
One hundred thousand to F S. Which one is that now? Three hundred to Satellite. Let's see the date.

GARBA

Weka, I vowed not to beat you, but don't push me! Now, will you give me back that cheque booklet at once! You are not an auditor in this house.

WEKA

Of course not. Only a slave. I am here to knit my fingers sore to clothe my children and pay for their education while you distribute all the money to prostitutes. Look at my shoes.

GARBA

Aren't they better than anything you ever had in the orphanage?

WEKA

The orphanage was the orphanage. Now I am supposed to be a wife. And not just any wife - one who brought you a lot of wealth. By marrying me - if one can call this marriage - you became lord and master over the cocoa farms and the oil palm estate my father left me.

GARBA

And now what?

WEKA

And now you harvest from them like a thief. No pruning of the trees, no weeding of the farms themselves, not even clearing the road thereto. And when you sell the produce, nobody sees where the proceeds go to. (*Sighs*) Anyway, I don't blame you. Here. (*slaps the book on the table*) Take your cheque booklet and do whatever you like with the money. If I ever ask you about it again, you can call me a dog. (*Rises*) I'll fetch your food...if you care for any.

GARBA

No, thanks. I've had my feast of quarrelling. Now I must go.

WEKA

Where are you going?

GARBA

I have to meet a foreign supplier in Douala.

WEKA

Going to Douala, and this is when you tell me.
(*Phone rings*)

GARBA

That's the way you like it.

WEKA

When are you coming back?

GARBA

(Moving away)
Tomorrow morning.
(phone rings again)

WEKA

(picking up receiver)
Hello?
*(There is a hum as the phone is hung up at the other end. Weka
smiles and hangs up noisily).*

Curtain

✳ ✳ ✳

Scene 4

(At the theatre, prolonged applause as curtain rises).

IMPRESARIO

Thank you very much. You are wonderful. Thank you. Now let me
introduce the cast. King Herod, who had many wives but still seized
his brother's only wife, was played by Sama Samba. (*applause*) In
the role of Salome, the girl who asked for John's head on a platter
as a prize for her dancing, you had Fatima Shetu. (*applause*). And
last but not least, John the Baptist, who was beheaded because
he dared point out Herod's injustice toward his brother, Austin
Ngom! (*applause*). Thank you. (*applause continues*) Thank you.

You are a marvellous audience. We hope you enjoyed the play as much as we enjoyed playing for you on our opening night. You are all invited to our next performance which will be in the same hall in two weeks.

(*applause and screeching of chairs as the crowd rise to leave the hall. Garba and Fatou can be seen arm-in-arm in the crowd*).

GARBA

Nice play. Super performance. What do you say? (*Fatou is pale and does not answer*) What's wrong, Fatou? You suddenly became dumb....

FATOU

Ssssh. Look at the exit to our right. See the second couple in the crowd moving towards us? Nearest to the showcase?

GARBA

Oh my God! It's your husband. You said he did not care for theatre.

FATOU

Is that all you see?

GARBA

What? My wife, arm-in-arm with Sani at the theatre?

FATOU

(*Dragging him by the hand*) Come, let's disappear before they see us.

GARBA

Wait. Let go of my hand, Fatou. I must...I cannot understand how....

WEKA

(*Interrupting with a derisive laugh*) We shall all understand, Garba. I didn't know Douala was another name for Capitol Theatre.

GARBA
(Anger and shock in his voice)
What, in Allah's name, are you doing here, Weka?

WEKA
And what, in God's name, are you doing here, comrade PDG?

(Curtain falls as they are about to start a fight)

✳ ✳ ✳

ACT IV

Scene 1

(Weka's house - decrepit building in a piteous state of disrepair. Weka is scrubbing the ceiling with a long brush, Emeka walks in through open door).

EMEKA
Hm! Ashia for renovation work oh.

WEKA
Boh, lef me. I de trespass for spider and rat them territory. It's a shame there is no Agric show coming. My spiders and rats would win all the prizes.
(They laugh) Sorry, my hands are dirty.
(Pointing to a log of wood)
Please, make yourself...*(laugh)* I was going to say 'comfortable'. On a log of wood.

EMEKA
What are you talking about, Weka? Quich is more comfortable and more honourable - to sit on the bare floor for your own place or to bear insultation inside the palace of another somebody else?

WEKA
You are right, Emeka.
(Shakes his hand)
And to think of all I put into making a man of that...that pig.

EMEKA
The debit quich Garba owes you is opendential secret. And that apply to the beastly ungrateful ingratitude with quich he reward

45

you. And everybody who hear it is appalling by it. In fact myself I am very mad at you.

WEKA

Mad at me?

EMEKA

Honest to God.

WEKA

What about, honey?
 (Suppressing a laugh)

EMEKA

Weka, it is not laughing matter. Perhaps you thinks that I am still sore because you refuse to marry me twenty years ago. No, my proud have recover from that blow. But the thing quich is above my intelligent is how manage you prefer that...rusticated fool who now take liberty to treat you like...*(agitated)* like slave...like animal self. Honest, Weka it is more than my....

WEKA

(Taking it easy) Well, Emeka my dear, how could I have known, twenty years ago, that he would turn out so mean and beastly?

EMEKA

Very well, Weka. But how manage you tolerate that kind of...I call it rape, for twenty years? As if you have no choose - a lady of your calibration!

WEKA

Listen, Emeka, you had just about the same upbringing I had in the orphanage. So you of all should understand my predicament. Sister Sabeth told me that quite often it takes a good woman to pull a wayward man together. I don't pretend to be a good woman, but somehow that is the mini-miracle I have been trying all that long to bring about for Garba. But with a phenomenon like him, it's plain pointless.

EMEKA

(*Shakes his head*) Weka, you remember me of one proverb from the plateau tribe in Delta, quich say that good grass always grow where there is no cows. I swear that everything woul' have been different if...

WEKA

If I had married you instead, right? But I happen to know that you have had a succession of domestic struggles yourself in the past couple of years. And of the most violent and bloody kind, I'm told. Well, it could perhaps have been different with me, as you say, who knows? But that's quite another kettle of fish now. The milk has been spilt.

EMEKA

Why are you hurry haste to put full-stop when the two both of us are still alive and....

WEKA

Please, Emeka why don't we talk about something else?

EMEKA

What else for instance example? Okay, your children. Did you left them all behind?

WEKA

Crazy? So they could go on slaving away for his brood of bastards? No way. My children took straight off with me the same night of the scandal at the theatre.

EMEKA

But where are they now?

WEKA

Out in the forest, naturally. We didn't come here on a safari. Some are trying to rehabilitate the farm, others are fetching building materials. We have to build this place back into a respectable home.

EMEKA

All on your own?

WEKA

I had wanted to be on my own when I had to leave the orphanage twenty years ago. What more now that we are a family?

EMEKA

(*Smiles and pats her on the shoulder*) Yes, that's what Reverend Gordon used to call self-reliance. And I love it. That was first doctrine I give to my children too. Now they are captain for it. But I think Reverend Gordon must to help you. It is even by compulsory.

WEKA

Gordon and Sabeth owe us nothing. I guess they did all they knew how, or thought fit, while I was in the orphanage.

EMEKA

I say they did not do no nothing. Not enough anyhow. For you, for me, for Nyassa, for Jomo - for any child who growed up in that orphanage. Thas why after leaving, nobody looks back.

WEKA

You are perfectly right, Emeka. But my gratitude to them is based on the Chinese proverb that when you give a hungry child a fish, you feed him for one day, but....

EMEKA

But when you teaches him how to fish, you feeds him for the remaining balance of his life. I tell you, those Hing Hong people does not only know judo, karate and acrobat.

WEKA

The Chinks are sages without parallel. From morning to evening.

EMEKA

But since you left the orphanage, does you see Gordon at all?

WEKA

Not much. He is not particularly fond of Garba. But I hear of late he had been having compunctions about having let me off when he did. He is quoted as regretting that he underestimated the capacity of my late father's farms and lands.

EMEKA

Of course. He must bite his finger now.

WEKA

Especially when he sees all the boom sales of cocoa and palm oil Garba has been making off the farms.

EMEKA

Right. And especially now that the orphanage is empty and....

WEKA

And, as you said, none of the former inmates feels any obligation to support him. The once all-sufficient Gordon's sun is setting.

EMEKA

And I am sure he now want someone to lean on.

WEKA

Well, how much easier it would all have been for him if he had done like Louis!

EMEKA

Louis? Who is that?

WEKA

Oh, you don't know Louis? That's my foster father-in-law. You mean you don't know that Garba also grew up in an orphanage?

EMEKA

Oh yes. Of course I am do. And the rector of the orphanage was called Louis. That yeye man.

WEKA

And Louis taught Garba to feel like a member of his own family. To this day, even as an old polygamist and father of a brood of brats, Garba does nothing without asking Louis first. Would you believe, for instance, that Garba lets Louis keep his money for him and cannot buy anything without Louis' blessing?

EMEKA

Plus including money from your farms?

WEKA

Of course. I was his to do just as he pleased with. How much more so my property? But you have not heard the worst. When Garba sells anything, including palm oil and cocoa from my father's farms, the payment passes through Louis who lets him have only twenty percent of it.

EMEKA

No! Weka, tell me you are just funnicating.

WEKA

Making fun about something that serious. What do you take me for?

EMEKA

So what happen to the balance remainder of eighty percent?

WEKA

That's the punchline to the joke. Louis keeps it in his safe and from it he has been giving Garba high-interest loans whenever he needs to buy or build something.

EMEKA

Chineke meh!!! Loan! From my own money? That means Garba is worser than slave now. So what are he do about it?

WEKA

Nothing. And he is not alone. All those who grew up in Louis' orphanage are in the same predicament - Omar, Bedel, Nyasi, Sedar, Houpho, Tombal – all of them. The day Louis lets them have all their money, he will become a church rat.

EMEKA

Oh yes oh! Thas why any of them who have make any temptation to claim their rightful....

WEKA

Dare open your mouth, he promptly sends his thugs to quietly smother you, or if you are lucky to live, he declares someone else husband to your wives and father to your children. For speaking up, young Sanki paid with his life.

EMEKA

I beg, don't remember me of Sanki. His assassination killing is paining me till tomorrow. Any time I member him I feel like to start another world war.

WEKA

(Looking outside)
Ssssh! I see a white helmet coming. Looks like Gordon. He sent word he would be dropping in some time. Gosh, how he has aged!

EMEKA

Listen, Weka, I must go now. I am sure Gordon does not wants people to know that he come to see you here.

WEKA

Very nice and thoughtful of you, Emeka. But you don't have to slip off like that. If you don't want to meet Gordon, you can take a walk in the garden behind the house. You will have fun with the mice and lizards.
(shows him out through rear door) This way.
Emeka barely slips out, unseen by Gordon who enters with a cane. With him is Rican.

WEKA

How good to see you, Reverend Gordon! It's been ages.

GORDON

(Embraces her)
You look great, my dear. Especially after all what I heard. And let me introduce my friend.

JIM

(Shaking hands with Weka)
Hi! I am Jim Rican

WEKA

You are very welcome, Mr Rican.

JIM

You can just call me Jim.

WEKA

I think I've met you before. You are one of the customers of Garba's co-operative. Please, sit down, Jim. Anywhere you like.
(They all sit)

GORDON

Weka my dear, I meant to come before now - at least to apologise. I heard all about how Garba has been molesting you, and just cannot forgive myself for marrying you off to him in the first place.

WEKA

Nothing to feel guilty about, Reverend Gordon. You were not God to know he would turn out like that.

GORDON

No, I wasn't. But I think I should have maintained a certain presence. Maybe not exactly like Louis, but at least a dissuasive presence – to deter him, from his excesses.

WEKA

Come to think of it, it could have made a difference if he felt that I had someone behind me like he had Louis. But that's spilt milk now, isn't it? My immediate concern is to renovate this old house which my old man left behind, and to develop the property for my children.

GORDON

And that is precisely why I came. To see if I could be of help in any way.

WEKA

That's ever so nice of you, Reverend Gordon. I will rally my boys once they are all here, so we can determine those things we can do ourselves, and those we need help with.

GORDON

Rehabilitating your farms, for example, protecting them from any further plunderers, training your children in various fields - anything I can do.

JIM

I can also lend a hand with just anything you want. You name it, and I....

WEKA

Garba told me you were a gunsmith.

JIM

Ah, his phobia for guns! I make and sell a whole lot of other things. Why does everyone always think of the guns first?

WEKA

Well, what we really need more urgently is food - which we can produce ourselves. We also need clothes and medicine and a nice big house on this foundation.

JIM

Yes, and as I said, I supply all those things and more. Plus, you cannot rule out guns completely. You will need to defend your farm against usurpers like Garba, and to shoot monkeys when they come to steal your cocoa pods. You may also have covetous neighbours who could toy with taking advantage of the smallness of your family and of the fact that there is no man behind you.

WEKA

This is very true, Jim. But to buy guns, or anything for that matter, we need money, which we can....

JIM

That's nothing to worry about. We know what you have been through. I'm sure I can lend you some. Really, that's no problem.

WEKA

Very kind of you, Jim. Just that I remember this little adage that he who goes a-borrowing....

JIM

Oh forget about going a-sorrowing. You cannot expect to get by nowadays without borrowing or taking something on credit or hire-purchase.

WEKA

Way too early, Jim. Self-reliance first. Do you make and sell machetes and hoes by any chance?

JIM

Machetes and hoes? What a question! Everything you could ever need for your farm, including combine harvesters. Also, for the repairs on your house. In fact, I can have one made back in Memphis and assembled here.

WEKA

That's what you call a prefab, isn't it?

JIM

You got it.

WEKA

To be sincere, Jim, I think for now things like prefabs are out of the question. Just look through the window. See that vast forest, way across the foot of the mountain and right up to the plateau the other end. It's all mine. What do I do with all the Ebony, Iroko, Bilinga...you name the tree and it is found in that forest. My children will never forgive me if, instead of using the abundance of local building material, I went ordering prefabs. Maybe later.

JIM

That's alright. Any time.

GORDON

And do you have prospective buyers for your cocoa or do you plan to continue selling through Garba's cooperative?

WEKA

Reverend Gordon, the farms are all forest yet.

GORDON

But you need to think of a market before you start producing again.

WEKA

You are right, Reverend Gordon, but who says I will go on producing cocoa?

JIM

Why not? I can buy up whatever you produce.

WEKA

Jim, I must say it's been waiting too long for a friend like you to show up. But at what price would you buy?

JIM

Depends. About a million CFA per tonne. Good price, isn't it?

WEKA

Well...and for how long? And then if I compare that with what you charge for a bar of chocolate.... In fact, Jim, my children seem to think we should rather grow corn, yams and plantains. That way even if we can't sell our produce at any time, we can eat it, and help some hungry neighbours too.

GORDON

That makes sense, Weka. But you cannot leave out cocoa completely. You need to diversify your sources of revenue.

GARBA

(from outside)
Knock knock!

GORDON

(Amused, to Weka)
Interesting, this African habit of knocking with the mouth.

WEKA

Saves you having to ask who's there, since you can already tell from
the knocker's voice. More practical, isn't it?

GORDON

It certainly is. So who do you think is knocking now?

WEKA

Garba. Who else? Please, Rev. Gordon, I think you'd better go into
the garden. He's such a beast you never can tell what he'll come
up with. I would much rather he doesn't see you. Come this way.
(Shows them out through rear door)

GARBA

(Still from outside)
I say, is there no one here? Weka!
(knocks savagely on the door)

WEKA

(Going to open)
You don't have to knock my rickety door off its hinges, do you?
(Opens door and Garba enters).

GARBA

*(Stalking about and looking the house over with an air of
amusement)*
Hm, someone has been busy here. *(laughs)* Weka, you are funny,
very funny.

WEKA

(Cynical)
Am I not? *(pause)* Look, I've got things to do. What do you want?

GARBA

What I want? I want you to go home with me. Whatever your grievances, they are no excuse for you to run off and live in this... ramshackle....

WEKA

That ramshackle is where I was born. And it's a shame I did not come back to it straight from the orphanage. But that's the past. Now I'm back and another step out of here is plain out of the question.

GARBA

That's a joke, Weka. You are going back with me.

WEKA

(Laughs)
Am I? Well, go bring all your brethren, and a stretcher, or better still, a bulldozer.

GARBA

Look, I don't want to lose my temper again. I expect you to be reasonable.

WEKA

Garba my dear friend, I expect you to understand that it is over with. *(Shouts)* I expect you to leave! Now!

GARBA

Weka, you are shouting at me!

WEKA

Garba, I have every right to shout or do whatever I like here. Just you go away. You have no business here. Between you and me, it's finished! Why can't you grasp it? Are you so thick....

GARBA

(*Smacks her*)

Shut up! And now...(*hustling her*) let's see if you won't go with me.

WEKA

Garba, you have slapped me; now please, let go of me.

GARBA

(*Still hustling her*) Come on! You'll go, Right now!

WEKA

(*Resisting forcefully, shouts*)

Help! Help! Help!)

Enter Emeka, Gordon and Jim.

EMEKA

What's going on here?

GORDON

Garba, what's happening? Has it come to this?

JIM

What a shame!

GARBA

You are all here!

(*Nods his head*)

I see. (*Pause*) But my business is with my wife. Now (*pushes Weka*) Going, you slut!

EMEKA

(*Intervening*) Thas no way to treat a lady, Miché Garba. Do you have no shame?

GARBA

You again! It was you who had the guts to perturb our wedding. You walked right up in church and said....

EMEKA

And I still says it; that with this bastard fashion you don't deserve lady like Weka.

GARBA

Emeka my friend, watch what you say or do here. Twenty years ago, you were a rival suitor to a spinster from an orphanage. Today you are meddling in a couple's private affairs.

EMEKA

It can be private affair of Governor-general himself. But you cannot be brutal for her in my present.

GARBA

Get out of my way, Emeka. You are looking for trouble. Reverend Gordon, please, advise him if he is your friend.

GORDON

Well, but why are you trying to use force? It was of her free will she accepted you twenty years ago.

EMEKA

Aha! there comes your.... What you call it? Freewheel? Are you forgot what I told you?

GARBA

(To Gordon)
And it was you who gave her to me...for better or for worse.

JIM

Yes, but if she has had enough of the relationship; if it turned out different than what she hoped for, she is not bound to stay on.

The courts and even the Bible allow for divorce in cases where....

GARBA

Oh, I see. She's got all the pocket solicitors and advocates. I understand.... But I'll get back to you all yet. For now, (*turning to Weka*) my business is with you.
   (*Grabs her by her collar and her sleeve*)
Come on!

WEKA

Leave me alone. I am not moving one inch. And if you don't go away before my children come back, you'll be sorry you ever...
   Enter children

AKO

What's happening here?

2ND CHILD

Leave mama alone!

GARBA

Shut up, children. I am your father and you must all come home with me. Now!

AKO

We are not going anywhere unless mama says so. And in any case, you cannot force us.

GARBA

Ako, come here.
   (*grabs his arm and twists it.*)
Who are you talking to like that?

WEKA

Enough, Garba. You have been brutal to me and got away with it because I had accepted to be your...your...slave. But don't you lay a finger on one of my children. You will have to bury me ...

GARBA

They are my children you are talking about, woman.

WEKA

You have no family here. Go away! Get out!

CHILDREN

(*together*) Yes, go away! We don't want you.

GARBA

Children, you'll be sorry for all this.

AKO

Now, Mr. Miché Garba, let's end this joke here. Look, we are just
back from the forest and
(*holds up his cutlass and looks at his brethren who do the
same*)
... and you can see our cutlasses are quite handy and keen. But
we don't want blood. So take my advice and leave.
(*threatening*)
Immediately!

GARBA

Are you all gone crazy? Look! I order you to...

AKO

Order who? Now, out with you!

CHILDREN

(*Together*)
Get out! Go away! Leave us alone!
(*They fall on him and push him out.*)

ACT V

Scene 1

(*Courtroom*).

JUDGE
You can sit down, Mr. Garba. Now, Mrs. Weka Garba, how do you...

WEKA
Your Worship, my name is Weka. Garba is out of the question.

JUDGE
(*Smiles*) And how do you plead to the charges preferred against you by Miché Garba, your husband, for abandoning your conjugal home?

WEKA
Not guilty, your Worship. I want this court to know that Garba and I are not, and never were, formally married.

GARBA
(*Bursts into laughter*) Do you hear that, Your Worship? This woman has gone crazy.

JUDGE
Miché Garba, you are reminded for the last time that you are in a court of law. This talking out of turn shall cease with immediate effect.

GARBA
Yes, Sir.

JUDGE

(*To Garba*) And since you want to talk, what evidence do you have that this woman, Weka, is legally your wife?

GARBA

Thank you, Sir. Rev. Gordon and Sister Sabeth, in whose care she grew up, and who gave her in marriage to me, are both present in this court. So is Rev. Unor, the minister who solemnised our marriage, and Kinge, my comrade, who was our best man. They can all attest to the legality of our marriage.

JUDGE

Let all those who have been cited as witnesses in this case, please, leave the room. Except Kinge who shall immediately take the witness box. (*Kinge takes the box*) Take the Bible in your right hand and say after me...I, Kinge Dibum, (*He repeats*) swear to tell the truth..... the whole truth..... and nothing but the truth...... so help me, God.

KINGE

Comrade Miché is my Union boss. And it was just before our final campaign rally twenty years ago that he broke the news to me and I, in turn, broke it to the Union convention – that he was taking for himself another wife. And, naturally, I was present in church when the marriage was solemnised by (*bows towards Unor*) Reverend Unor here present. Since then, Comrade Miché and Madam lived happily together – until recently, when she suddenly left home. As far as I am concerned, they are still husband and wife. Every couple has its ups and downs.

JUDGE

Kinge, no one asked you to substitute yourself for the judge in this court. (*To Weka*) Now, Madam, do you have any questions for the witness?

WEKA

None, Your Worship.

JUDGE

You may retire, Mr. Kinge. Please, call in the other witnesses - Rev. Gordon and Sister Sabeth. (*Enter Sabeth and Gordon as Kinge disappears into the crowd*).

JUDGE

Reverend Gordon, this court has been told that it was you who gave this woman in marriage to this man.

GORDON

Yes, in fulfilment of a promise I made to her mother when she handed her over to us as an orphan.

JUDGE

And you are sure it was to this man, Miché Garba, and no other?

GORDON

Absolutely sure. However, Your worship...

JUDGE

That will do. Does the accused have any questions?

WEKA

If your Worship does not mind, I would like to defer all questioning until I have heard all the witnesses.

JUDGE

The accused's request is granted. (*To Gordon and Sabeth*) You may retire. And now let the court hear Rev. Unor. (*Unor takes the box*).

JUDGE

You wedded this woman to this man twenty years ago, is that true?

UNOR

True.

JUDGE

Can you briefly recount the circumstances?

UNOR

Twenty years is a long time, Your Worship. But I remember that em… em… Emekwachu…someone with an impossible name, came up with a claim. He said Weka was his wife.

JUDGE

And what did you say or do?

UNOR

He could not quite back up his claims. In fact he spoke some mumbo-jumbo we could not make head or tail of. So we could not help ignoring him.

JUDGE

Does the defendant want to ask her questions now?

WEKA

Yes, Your Worship. My first question goes to Rev. Gordon and Sister Sabeth. Please, tell the court what was my attitude up to the moment I was being led to the altar.

SABETH

In truth, Your Worship, Weka kept protesting to marrying what she insisted was a complete stranger. When all attempts at persuasion failed, we kind of coerced her – because she had reached the age at which her mother had insisted we should give her in marriage.

JUDGE

Is the witness telling this court in substance that the woman did not marry the man of her own free will?

SABETH

In a way, yes, Your Worship. Her preference at the time was to be allowed to be on her own. But we thought that would expose her to too many odds.

WEKA

Now a question for Rev. Unor. In solemnising this ... simulation ... you asked me the customary question, namely if I accepted Garba as my wedded husband... for better or for worse... and so on and so forth. Would you tell the court my response?

UNOR

She said nothing for a very long time. In fact, she burst into tears. But as she had to be married off according to her mother's will, we consulted with her foster parents and then proceeded to solemnise the marriage on condition.

JUDGE

What was the condition?

UNOR

That Weka and Garba would live as husband and wife for ten years, during which time they would get to know each other better. After this she was to be given a final chance to choose between maintaining the status quo and relinquishing the arrangement.

JUDGE

In other words, what you solemnised was not really a marriage but a kind of official concubinage, on the basis of a compatibility test. Is that correct?

UNOR

The way Your Worship puts it makes it all sound like a farce of sorts. But in truth, that is what we did. It was a kind of simulation. You see, we were hard put to pronouncing a final marriage without the express consent of one of the parties.

JUDGE

Was this condition written in the marriage register?

UNOR

Yes, by my own hand, Your worship.

JUDGE

And what matrimonial arrangement was it – I mean apart from being on probation?

UNOR

What a question! We are Christian ministers, and could only solemnise monogamy, Your Worship.

JUDGE

Now, after the probationary period was over, did you officially seek Weka's opinion as stipulated in the solemnisation act?

UNOR

By signing the register Garba had accepted this condition. And when the time came, he asked to be trusted with organising the consultation. Well, up till that time we had heard no complaint from Weka; which, to us, meant that there was no real trouble, and that the consultation was thus going to be a mere formality. So, we had no objection to letting Garba handle it as head of the family, it being understood that we would step in at once if the need arose.

JUDGE

And it seems this need never arose.

UNOR

Nothing serious was brought to our attention, Your Worship.

JUDGE

Does the defendant have any further questions for the witnesses?

WEKA

None for now, Your Worship.

GARBA

My wife and I had no problem, Your Worship. And so, as Reverend Gordon said, it was only a formality. The family simply came together and celebrated the tenth anniversary of our marriage, unanimously pledging to stay happily together ever after.

JUDGE

Would you tell the court what you mean by "family"?

GARBA

By "family" I mean Weka and her children, as well as my other wives and their children.

WEKA

You have heard, Your Worship. He has just admitted that he had other wives, some before I came to him, others after. And yet during the solemnisation he signed for monogamy. The court has certainly taken note that I was entrapped unwittingly into a polygamous marriage.

JUDGE

But when you settled in with him, and noticed this deceit, it seems you did not raise a finger either.

WEKA

It did not quite bother me then. Actually, I did not quite move in with him then, since I did not live under his roof. I stayed in my late father's premises, and this is where he came to me whenever he wanted me. This means I did not get a chance to know too much about him and his other women. And when I got to know, I felt there was no need to protest before the end of the common-law status.

JUDGE

But that status ended without incident, and now...

WEKA

Your Worship must not forget that Garba knew it was a probation period. So he was generally meek, friendly and foxy. He spoilt my children with little presents – and that can have an effect on a woman who grew up in an orphanage and only knew a life of frugality.

And then, come the final consultation day, he brings us all together – with his other women – and throws a lavish party to fete our ten years together. In the heat of the euphoria he rises and harangues the assembly:

"We're all a happy family, aren't we?" And all those women, some of them quite drunk, answer with a deafening "yes, we are", and burst out ululating.

"We shall continue to be one, indivisible and happy family, shan't we?" he goes on. And they all hoot back, "yes we shall".

"Thank you all, my wives and children" he says, beaming with satisfaction. "Now, confirm what you just said by raising your hand". And the throng, including guests, raised their hands, and he counted them all.

GARBA

I don't know about outsiders being counted, Your Worship, but ask her if she did not raise her hand.

WEKA

I did, Your Worship, because I did not want to be a wet blanket, secondly because my not doing so would have made no difference anyway, since it was now a matter of numbers and my voice and my children's would be drowned by that of the crowd. The real issue here, Your Worship, is that there was no provision in the solemnisation act for consulting other women – since, in principle, there were no other women. The provision was for me to declare if I wanted to continue or stop living with him. But this arrangement drowned my voice completely. In any case, I thought it was alright as long as we'd live on as before – that is under separate roofs. But once the festivities were over...

GARBA

So you expected us, as husband and wife, to continue living miles apart indefinitely, with me being only a regular visitor – just like a lover?

WEKA

If I may go on, Your Worship...

JUDGE

Yes, go on.

WEKA

Once the festivities were over, he brought a fleet of trucks and bundled my children and me out of our house. His drivers gathered all our stuff, trampling and damaging many things etc... and so he forced me to settle in with him. Thenceforth he took to forcing my children to learn his mother tongue and forget mine with which they were raised. I have had to abide by the customs of his clan, not mine, and ... in short he has simply been breathing down my neck since then.

GARBA

Your Worship, this hearing seems to me to have drifted away from the point at issue – namely that my wife has abandoned her con-jugal home.

JUDGE

It is not the place of the plaintiff, or any party for that matter, to determine what the court shall or shall not hear. Has the defend-ant finished?

WEKA

Your Worship, I deem it pointless to go into further detail. I am
sure that the gross abuses and irregularities of this relationship
are clear enough for the court to decide, in total independence,
whether it is humanly possible to consider it a marriage and sus-
tain it as such.

GARBA

If I understand her well, Weka is asking for divorce.

WEKA

By your leave, Your Worship, (*then to Garba*) for that to happen,
my dear friend, there has to have been legal marriage. What I am
saying is that ours was a relationship too fraught with deceit and
irregularities to be considered marriage. In simple language, I am
saying that we are not married.

JUDGE

Does the plaintiff have anything further to say or any questions
to ask?

GARBA

Nothing, Your Worship.

JUDGE

This case stands adjourned.

Court rises as curtain falls

❋ ❋ ❋

Scene 2

Garba's Office. He is discussing with Kinge.

GARBA

Kinge, my dear, you must find me a secretary, quick.

KINGE

That will be quite easy. But you must not expect one as good as Fatou.

GARBA

Forget about Fatou. Her husband has forced her to resign. You know after the incident at the Capitol…

KINGE

But I hope you have not stopped seeing her, Comrade Garba. Of all your girls Fatou was the one with the most class. The most discreet too.

GARBA

Let's forget Fatou for a while. I've got too much to grapple with. On the domestic front, this thing with Weka seems to be having a snowball effect. Every day now there is another of my wives packing to go away. I can't sleep a wink. Twenty-four hours a day I am talking, pleading, begging them to stay.

KINGE

Comrade, how can you be begging women to stay when there are young, fresh, full-breasted things all about, ready to climb up your window? If they go, they will be the ones to regret, not you.

GARBA

You miss the point, Kinge. They are not such fools after all. It is all blackmail. I hope so. And if it is, the timing is perfect. If they were to leave now, while this case with Weka is still on, do you imagine the conclusions the court would draw?

KINGE

Yes, I see. How short-sighted I was!

GARBA

And then you seem to be dreaming on our past glories. Even in business the going has got atrociously tough. Look at that. (*Hands him a letter*) That's the fifth of my foreign partners in a row to cancel orders in two months. What will the cooperative do with the excess cocoa? And once the farmers can't get paid, it's my position as General Manager of the Cooperative that's on the line. And no full-breasted things would be climbing up the window of a...

KINGE

Of course, not. I see with you. But it's not as immediate as that, I hope. At least the farmers can be paid from the reserves of the previous year's sale while hoping that the market situation improves.

GARBA

Kinge, you have been my closest aide in both party and business, and you talk like an outsider. (*Searches for a bank statement and shoves it across to Kinge*) Look at that statement. Your Cooperative account. It's dated yesterday.

KINGE

(*Shocked*) Dated yesterday, and in red! How come?
(*There is a knock at the door*).

GARBA

Come in.
	Enter Sani
Ah! It's you. Please, sit down. I was just about to send Comrade Kinge to see you.

SANI

Oh yeah? Of what help can I be to the...

GARBA

Sani, I want you back. I need a driver I can rely on. I will double your pay if only...

SANI

Excuse me, Mr. Garba, but I came here on an errand. (*Hands him a police summons*)

GARBA

(*Stunned on reading it*) What? A police summons? For what now?

KINGE

It never rains but it pours. Sani, why are you doing this? After all, I thought the offences cancelled out. You caught Comrade Garba with your wife, and he caught you with his.

SANI

Well, Comrade Garba reserves the right to file a suit against me as well. It's a matter of who has something to lose.

GARBA

(*Going on his knees*) Please, Sani, don't do this to me. Not now, in Allah's name. Please, I'll give you whatever...

SANI

(*Leaving*) Excuse me, Mr. Garba. It's for the police to decide now.

KINGE

But you can withdraw your complaint, Sani.

GARBA

Withdraw it, Sani, please.

SANI

Too late, Sir. (*Slams the door as he exits*)

Curtain

✳ ✳ ✳

Scene 3

(*Court Room*).

JUDGE

In the case of Miché Garba versus Weka, the jury has come to the following decision:

Taking cognizance of the concordant evidence rendered by the prosecution witnesses, it is fair to conclude that there was marriage between plaintiff and respondent, as per entry No. 001/UN of February 11, 1961.

(*Garba and his wives burst into jubilation.*)

Silence, please! A woman cannot stay with a man for twenty years and argue that there was no marriage. (*more jubilation from Garba and his people*)

Under these circumstances the jury upholds the plaintiff's claim that his wife is liable to damages for abandoning him.

GARBA

(*Jubilant*) Long live Your Worship!

JUDGE

However, considering the immediate circumstances which led to the defendant's flight, namely a fight resulting from a potentially scandalous affair of mutual infidelity – or suspicion thereof – about which both parties have been noticeably silent during this hearing; the jury is of the opinion that the flight was a perfectly natural reaction. (*Garba is quiet and wears a grin*)

That the plaintiff resorted to court action rather than to an attempt to reason and reconcile with his spouse, also seems to the jury, to confirm the lovelessness of the relationship between the couple, and hence the permanent instability of the marriage. (*Dead silence*)

Furthermore, given that the solemnisation act quoted heretofore provided for monogamy, whereas the plaintiff has publicly admitted to having other wives;

Also, inasmuch as the same act, which is the only legal sanction for the said marriage, allowed for the couple to live in physical separation though united in what has been described as 'simulated wedlock';

And finally, given that, at the confirmation of the marriage following the compatibility test, voices other than that of the concerned party were enlisted, and that these voices influenced the outcome of the said consultation;

The court decides as follows:

One - that the marriage remains subject to confirmation between husband and wife, on a one-to-one basis, and to the total exclusion of all other parties. It shall become void once any one of the two parties concerned objects thereto.

Two - That pending the confirmation to be arranged at the couple's convenience, but strictly under the supervision of this court, the couple shall continue to live in physical separation under the same condition provided for in the probation by the solemnisation act.

(*Weka and her children and friends jump and shout for joy*).

And finally, three – that the couple are under injunction to be of good conduct towards each other, as cases of invective, infidelity, abuse or any form of scandal will lead to a regrettable intervention on the part of the court. This case is closed.

Shouts of joy from Weka and a host of her friends as the curtain falls.

The End

Victor Epie'Ngome was born on October 10, 1947, in Muabi, a small village in Cameroon's Muanenguba highlands. After primary education in RCM School, Muabi and Ave Maria School, Bangem, Epie was admitted into St. Joseph's College, Sasse. He later read Agriculture in CCAST Bambili and then Journalism, English Language and Linguistics at the University of Yaounde, Cameroon's only university at the time. His journalism studies included a stint at the University of Western Ontario in London, Canada, and Michigan State University in Lansing, Michigan.

As a journalist, Victor rose to Editor-in-Chief and TV Broadcast supervisor for Cameroon Radio Television - a career that put him at odds with the seamy side of state media policy, earning him a night with other colleagues in the Kondengi maximum security prison, and what he refers to as ten years in the garage - years when, for insisting on telling it as it is, he was paid but not allowed to work. During that time, he covered Cameroon for the BBC and later became a producer in Bush House as well as editor, writer or publisher for several newspapers and magazines. Upon retiring from active journalism, he took up media consultancy and training, alongside Civil Society activism in matters of governance, for which he founded an NGO called CIDI. Epie'Ngome is married and has three sons and two daughters.

ABOUT THE PUBLISHER

Spears Books is an independent publisher dedicated to providing innovative publication strategies with emphasis on African/ Africana stories and perspectives. As a platform for alternative voices, we prioritize the accessibility and affordability of our titles in order to ensure that relevant and often marginal voices are represented at the global marketplace of ideas. Our titles – poetry, fiction, narrative nonfiction, memoirs, reference, travel writing, African languages, and young people's literature – aim to bring African worldviews closer to diverse readers. Our titles are distributed in paperback and electronic formats globally by African Books Collective.

Connect with Us: Go to www.spearsmedia.com to learn about exclusive previews and read excerpts of new books, find detailed information on our titles, authors, subject area books, and special discounts.

Subscribe to our Free Newsletter: Be amongst the first to hear about our newest publications, special discount offers, news about bestsellers, author interviews, coupons and more! Subscribe to our newsletter by visiting www.spearsmedia.com

Quantity Discounts: Spears Books are available at quantity discounts for orders of ten or more copies. Contact Spears Books at orders@spearsmedia.com.

Host a Reading Group: Learn more about how to host a reading group on our website at www.spearsmedia.com

Printed in the United States
by Baker & Taylor Publisher Services